EP

# A Kid's Guide to Drawing™

# How to Draw Cartoon Holiday Symbols

Curt Visca and Kelley Visca

The Rosen Publishing Group's
PowerKids Press™
New York

*Dedicated to our daughter, Chloe, who enjoys every holiday*

Published in 2004 by The Rosen Publishing Group, Inc.
29 East 21st Street, New York, NY 10010

First Edition

Editor: Natashya Wilson
Book Design: Kim Sonsky
Layout Design: Michael J. Caroleo

Illustration Credits: All illustrations © Curt Visca.
Photo Credits: Cover and pp. 8, 10, 12, 18 © Index Stock Imagery, Inc.; p. 6 © Getty Images, Inc.; p. 14 © Phil Schermeister/CORBIS; p. 16 © Roy Morsch/CORBIS; p. 20 photograph by Michael J. Caroleo.

Visca, Curt.
  How to draw cartoon holiday symbols / Curt Visca and Kelley Visca. — 1st ed.
    p. cm. — (A kid's guide to drawing)
  Summary: Provides facts about eight holidays, as well as step-by-step instructions for drawing cartoons of symbols associated with each one.
  Includes bibliographical references and index.
  ISBN 0-8239-6726-3 (library binding)
  1. Drawing—Technique—Juvenile literature.  2. Holiday decorations in art—Juvenile literature.  3. Cartooning—Technique—Juvenile literature.   [1. Cartooning—Technique. 2. Drawing—Technique. 3. Holidays in art.]   I. Visca, Kelley. II. Title. III. Series.
  NC825.H65V57 2004
  741.5—dc21

  2002009021

# CONTENTS

# Cartoon Holiday Symbols

A holiday is a special day that celebrates a famous person or time in history. The word "holiday" comes from the words "**holy** day." Many holidays celebrate religious events. A holiday is often celebrated with decorations, parades, costumes, foods, and time off from either school or work.

In this book, you will learn about the history of eight holidays that are celebrated every year. Then you'll learn how to draw a cartoon **symbol** of each holiday. These cartoon drawings **animate** both people and objects. Sometimes you will draw eyes, a nose, and a mouth on things that aren't really alive, such as a valentine heart, to make them come to life. You will add action lines to make your drawings look as if they are moving. These cartoon drawings are kept simple. They include only the important lines and shapes. The details you add will make your cartoon drawings fun!

As you draw cartoon holiday symbols, you will develop your own cartooning style, or way of drawing. This may make your drawings look different from the ones in the book. That's great! Your style will set your drawings apart from everyone else's. You can be creative and add different features to your cartoon drawings. You can also **exaggerate** the features shown in this book.

You will need the following supplies to draw the holiday symbols:

- Paper
- A sharp pencil or a felt-tipped marker
- An eraser
- Colored pencils or crayons to add color

Choose a desk, a table, or another quiet place where you can draw your cartoons. Make sure that you have plenty of light and all your supplies nearby.

The directions under each drawing step will help you to add each new part to your cartoon. New parts are shown in red. The drawing shapes and terms are shown in the Terms for Drawing Cartoons on page 22.

Remember to work slowly, do your best, and practice your cartoons. Soon you'll be celebrating your success as a cartoonist along with these holidays. Turn the page and get ready to draw cartoon holiday symbols!

# Valentine's Day

Valentine's Day, February 14, honors Saint Valentine. It has become a day to celebrate love. Many people send cards and gifts to their sweethearts and friends. About 900 million cards, 103 million roses, and 35 million heart-shaped boxes of candy are bought around the world. Valentine symbols include hearts, candy, **Cupid**, and flowers. There are **legends** about how Valentine's Day began. Two Saint Valentines were priests in the third century. One priest is said to have married couples in secret after Roman emperor Claudius II made marriage against the law. The other priest was loved by many. When he was put in jail for his religious beliefs, children and friends who missed him threw notes into his jail cell. This may have started the **tradition** of sending notes on Valentine's Day. Legend says that Valentine was put to death on February 14, A.D. 269. Saint Pope Gelasius I made this day Valentine's Day in A.D. 496.

**1**

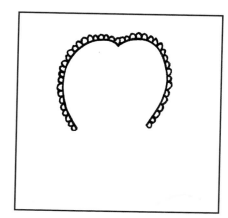

Let's draw a funny cartoon valentine! Start by making two curved lines for the top of the heart. Add small, upside-down letter *U*'s on the outside edge of each curved line.

**2**

Beautiful! Draw a letter *V* for the bottom of the heart. Add more letter *U*'s to complete the heart.

**3**

Draw two lines for the arm. Make curved lines for the thumb and ovals for the fingers. Use straight lines to start the flowers. Draw circles and teardrops for the flower tops.

**4**

Make the other arm and thumb. Start the box with a square. Draw crossed lines inside it. Add straight lines for the sides. Shade in squares for chocolates.

**5**

Super work! Draw two lines for each leg. Make an oval for each foot.

**6**

Make circles with dots inside for eyes. Add a curved nose. Make a smiling mouth and a caption. Lovely!

# St. Patrick's Day

St. Patrick's Day is celebrated on March 17, in honor of the **patron saint** of Ireland, Saint Patrick. He traveled to Ireland in the fifth century and spent 40 years teaching the Irish about **Christianity**. He used the three leaves of the **shamrock**, a type of clover, to explain the three parts of the **Trinity**. The shamrock became a symbol of St. Patrick's Day.

**Leprechauns** are also symbols of St. Patrick's Day. Irish legend tells that a leprechaun is an unfriendly little shoemaker who has hidden a pot of gold. If you catch a leprechaun, he will tell you where his gold is hidden. If you look away from him, he will disappear.

The first St. Patrick's Day celebration in the United States was held in Boston in 1737. Today people celebrate St. Patrick's Day with parades and by wearing green, the national color of Ireland.

**1**

Make two curved lines and two straight lines for the hat's brim. Draw three lines for the top of the hat. Add two squares for the buckle and four straight lines for the strap.

**2**

Under the hat, draw two short lines, curved lines for ears, and a letter *U* for the jaw. Draw circles with dots for the eyes. Add the nose and mouth. Make curved lines for the beard.

**3**

Fantastic job! Draw three straight lines for each sleeve. Make two curved lines for the stomach. Make two rectangles for a belt buckle. Add two ovals for buttons.

**4**

You are talented! Make rectangles for cuffs at the end of the sleeves. Draw five curved lines for fingers on each hand. Add curved lines inside to show the palms.

**5**

Draw two bent lines for the belt. Make a wavy curved line for the pants. Draw rectangles for boot buckles. Add two short lines and a sideways letter *V* for each boot.

**6**

Draw a pot of gold and a rainbow. Add ovals for gold coins. Add detail and action lines. Wow!

# Easter

Christians around the world celebrate Easter to remember the **resurrection**, or the return to life, of Jesus Christ after he died on the cross. Christians believe that they, too, will live after death, through their belief in Christ.

Spring begins around March 21 each year. Easter is celebrated on the Sunday after the following full moon. Many of the symbols of Easter stand for spring and new life. These symbols include chicks, lambs, bunnies, and eggs. Many children decorate eggs for Easter. On Easter morning, kids look for eggs hidden by the Easter bunny. Many children receive baskets filled with chocolate, jellybeans, and other goodies. In the United States, about 60 million chocolate bunnies and 15 million jellybeans are produced for Easter each year. If the jellybeans were lined up end to end, they would circle Earth almost three times!

1

Make ovals and dots for the eyes. Add eyebrows. Shade in a circle for the nose. Make a curved line with a teardrop inside for each ear. Draw curved lines for the head.

2

Add two letter U's for the mouth. Make short straight lines for teeth. Add shading underneath them. Draw three curved lines for the cheeks and chin. Make whiskers!

3

Draw a bent line and two straight lines for the arm. Make four curved lines for fingers. Add a curved line for the Easter egg. Decorate the egg however you like!

4

Awesome! Make a curved line and a bent line for the stomach and waist. Add a line for the back. Make two sideways letter V's for the other arm.

5

Draw straight lines for the shorts. Make two straight lines for the left leg and two curved lines for the right leg. Add curved lines for the feet. Make a fluffy tail using curved lines.

6

Add action lines and detail. Make grass from zigzag lines. Draw another Easter egg!

11

# Independence Day

U.S. citizens celebrate Independence Day each year on July 4. On this holiday, they remember July 4, 1776, the day that the Declaration of Independence was signed. This paper states that the United States is its own country, free from English rule.

On Independence Day, many Americans show their **patriotism**, or pride in their country. They decorate with red, white, and blue, the colors of the American flag. They have parades, picnics, and fireworks. Fireworks remind Americans of the battles fought during the **American Revolution** to free America from England.

The Chinese invented fireworks around A.D. 1000. Chemicals are mixed with metallic salts to create the bright colors, and metals such as aluminum give off white sparks and flashes. During a large fireworks display, 10,000 firework shells might be fired!

12

**1**

Let's begin by drawing a rectangle for the brim of the hat. Connect two bent lines for the hair on both sides. Add a wide letter U for the chin.

**2**

Draw three lines for the hat's top. Decorate it with stars and stripes! Make the eyes, nose, and mouth using circles, dots, curved lines, and straight lines. Shade in the mouth.

**3**

Very patriotic work! Make a letter U for the neck. Draw three straight lines for each sleeve. Make three straight lines for the rest of the shirt.

**4**

Draw two straight lines for each arm. Make a curved line for each thumb. Add three ovals on each hand for fingers. I salute you!

**5**

Make the shorts using straight lines. Draw two straight lines for each leg. Make a curved, sideways letter V for each shoe. Add curved lines to show the shoe tops.

**6**

Draw a flag in one hand and a sparkler in the other. Add action lines, "USA," and fireworks!

# Halloween

Halloween is celebrated on October 31. It is named for an ancient celebration called All Hallows' Eve. Many children carve pumpkins, dress up in scary or funny costumes, and go trick-or-treating on this holiday.

Pumpkins are popular Halloween symbols. People carve funny or scary faces into them, turning them into jack-o'-lanterns. The first jack-o'-lanterns were carved in Britain and Ireland, from beets, potatoes, and turnips. Irish legend tells of a man named Jack who had to wander Earth forever with a lantern made from a turnip. When the Irish came to America, they found more pumpkins than turnips and carved them instead.

The tradition of trick-or-treating probably came from All Souls' Day parades in England. On that day, poor people went door-to-door begging for food. In the United States, about $2 billion is spent on Halloween candy each year, more than is spent on candy for any other holiday.

**1**

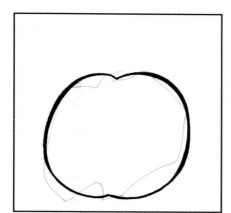

Start your cartoon jack-o'-lantern by connecting a letter C to a backward letter C.

**2**

Next make two straight lines and a curved line for the stem of the jack-o'-lantern.

**3**

Terrific work! Make an upside-down letter V for each eye. Add two straight lines and a curved line to complete each eye. Draw a triangle for the nose.

**4**

You are sensational! Next draw curved lines for the mouth, with three straight lines for each tooth.

**5**

Make a spider using an oval, two circles, two dots, curved lines, and one straight line. Draw a bat using straight lines and curved lines. Shade in both animals, leaving white spaces for their eyes.

**6**

Add shading and curved lines on the jack-o'-lantern. Make some grass. Add action lines. Spooky!

# Thanksgiving

On Thanksgiving, many American families gather to share a feast and give thanks for all the good things in their lives. The meal often includes turkey, stuffing, cranberry sauce, squash, mashed potatoes, and pumpkin pie. About 45 million turkeys are eaten in the United States on Thanksgiving Day.

The American Thanksgiving tradition is said to have started with the **Pilgrims** in 1621. They were thankful for their good harvest and feasted for three days. They were joined by about 90 Native Americans. Their meal included turkey, deer, corn, and squash. In 1789, President George Washington named November 26 a day of thanksgiving. In 1941, President Franklin D. Roosevelt made Thanksgiving a **federal** holiday, to be celebrated on the fourth Thursday in November.

**1**

Draw a circle and a letter C for the eyes. Shade in two circles for pupils. Make a curved line, a sideways letter V, and a short line for the beak. Add curved lines for the neck skin.

**2**

Draw a short line behind the eyes. Make a thin rectangle, two squares, another rectangle, and three lines for the hat. Add two bent lines for the head and neck.

**3**

Draw a curved line and straight lines for the collar. Make two rectangles for the buckle. Draw sideways letter V's for the shirt. Add a belt, then a straight line on the shirt.

**4**

You did it! Next make two lines for each sleeve. Draw three curved lines for each wing. Gobble gobble!

**5**

Start the pants with a short line on each side. Add straight lines for the legs. Finish with a curved line. Make shoes using bent lines and straight lines. Add heels. Draw tail feathers!

**6**

Add detail to show your turkey's feathers. Make eyebrows, buttons, and action lines. Super!

# Christmas

Christmas is celebrated on December 25 each year, to honor the birth of Jesus Christ. The word "Christmas" comes from the early English phrase *Cristes maesse*, or "Mass of Christ." For Christmas, many people set up **nativity** scenes that show

Christ's birth. Christmas has many traditional symbols. Saint Nicholas is said to have been a kind old man who gave gifts to the poor in European countries long ago. In the United States, he is called Santa Claus. People say he brings toys to good boys and girls on Christmas Eve. In the 1600s, the Germans began to decorate trees for Christmas. They used fruits, paper roses, and candles. Today, Americans buy more than 37 million live Christmas trees each year. Candy canes are another symbol of Christmas. About two billion candy canes are made each year.

**1**

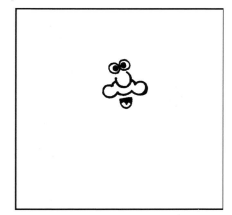

Let's start by making a circle and a dot for each eye. Draw a letter *U* for the nose. Connect curved lines for the mustache. Draw a mouth and shade it in.

**2**

Connect short curved lines to make the brim of Santa's hat. Add two long curved lines for its top. Make a puffball on the tip. Connect more curved lines for Santa's beard.

**3**

Make curved lines for Santa's belly. Add two straight lines for each arm, and use curved lines for each cuff. Draw rectangles for the belt and buckle. Add curved lines on Santa's shirt.

**4**

Next draw two lines and an upside-down letter *U* for the pants. Add curved lines at the bottom. Draw straight lines and letter *V*'s for Santa's boots. Add rectangles for buckles.

**5**

Use curved lines to draw Santa's mittens. Draw a large balloon shape for Santa's bag of toys. Add straight lines for the top. Make curved, straight, and thick lines for the candy cane.

**6**

Make crisscrossed lines and circles for snowflakes. Add detail and action lines. Ho ho ho!

# Hanukkah

Hanukkah is celebrated by Jewish people around the world. It begins on the twenty-fifth day of the Jewish month of Kislev, which usually falls in December. Hanukkah celebrates the **miracle** that is said to have occurred when Judah Maccabee **rededicated** the Jewish temple in Jerusalem in 165 B.C. The temple had been ruined by the king of Syria. To rededicate it, Maccabee needed a special oil to light the lamps. He found only enough for one night. However, the temple's lamps burned for eight nights! During Hanukkah, candles are lit on a **menorah** every night for eight nights to remember this miracle.

During the Hanukkah celebration, children play a game with a **dreidel**. Each of the dreidel's four sides is marked with a letter from the Hebrew alphabet. The letters stand for the phrase "A great miracle happened there." Children spin the dreidel. They win or lose chocolate, depending on which letter lands faceup.

**1**

Begin the last drawing by making an oval and a curved line for the eyes. Add a dot in each eye. Make a curved line for the nose. Draw curved lines for the mouth. Shade it in.

**2**

Super job! Draw five straight lines in a diamond shape for the side of the dreidel. Make two straight lines, an oval, and a curved line for the spinner.

**3**

Next draw a straight line and a sideways letter V for the top of the dreidel.

**4**

Make two straight lines for the left side of the dreidel. Draw a thick straight line and two thick curved lines to make the Hebrew letter *Nun*.

**5**

I am proud of your effort! Next make a large letter V for the bottom of the dreidel.

**6**

Draw curved lines to make the dreidel look as if it's spinning. Add zigzag lines for shading.

21

# Terms for Drawing Cartoons

Here are some of the words and shapes that you need to know to draw cartoon holiday symbols:

| | | | |
|---|---|---|---|
| ╭╭ | Action lines | V | Letter V |
| ⌐╮ | Bent lines | ◯ | Oval |
| ◯ | Caption | ▭ | Rectangle |
| ◯ | Circle | ● | Shading |
| ✳ | Crisscrossed lines | □ | Square |
| ⌒ | Curved line | ★ | Star |
| Ɛ∴ᵕᵕ | Detail | ☰ | Straight lines |
| ∴∴ | Dots | ◌ | Teardrop |
| C | Letter C | — | Thick line |
| U | Letter U | △ | Triangle |
| | | ⩘ | Zigzag lines |

# Glossary

**American Revolution** (uh-MER-ih-ken reh-vuh-LOO-shun)  Battles that soldiers from the colonies fought against Britain for freedom, from 1775 to 1783.

**animate** (A-nih-mayt)  To give life to.

**Christianity** (kris-chee-A-nih-tee)  A religion based on the teachings of Jesus Christ and the Bible.

**Cupid** (KYOO-pid)  The Roman god of love, usually shown as a winged boy with a bow and arrow.

**dreidel** (DRAY-dul)  A four-sided top with one Hebrew letter on each side, used to play Hanukkah games.

**exaggerate** (eg-ZA-juh-rayt)  To stretch beyond the truth.

**federal** (FEH-duh-rul)  Having to do with the central government.

**holy** (HOH-lee)  Blessed; important for reasons of faith.

**legends** (LEH-jendz)  Stories, passed down through the years, that cannot be proven.

**leprechauns** (LEP-ruh-konz)  Elves from Irish fairy tales.

**menorah** (meh-NOR-uh)  A candleholder with seven or nine candles used in the Jewish faith.

**miracle** (MEER-uh-kul)  A wonderful or an unusual event said to have been done by God.

**nativity** (nuh-TIH-vuh-tee)  A scene showing the birth of Jesus Christ.

**patriotism** (PAY-tree-uh-tih-zum)  Pride in one's country.

**patron saint** (PAY-trun SAYNT)  A special saint who is thought to help an individual, a trade, a place, a group, or an activity.

**Pilgrims** (PIL-grumz)  The people who sailed on the *Mayflower* in 1620 from England to America in search of freedom to practice their own beliefs.

**rededicated** (ree-DEH-dih-kayt-ed)  Set apart for a special use again.

**resurrection** (reh-zuh-REK-shun)  Coming back to life after dying.

**shamrock** (SHAM-rok)  A clover leaf with three leaflets.

**symbol** (SIM-bul)  An object or a design that stands for something else.

**tradition** (truh-DIH-shun)  A way of doing something that has been passed down over time.

**Trinity** (TRIH-neh-tee)  The Christian belief that the Father, the Son, and the Holy Spirit are three different things, but are also one being.

# Index

# Web Sites

Due to the changing nature of Internet links, PowerKids Press has developed an online list of Web sites related to the subject of this book. This site is updated regularly. Please use this link to access the list: www.powerkidslinks.com/kgd/holidays/